Beneath the Surface

D1312549

Rebecca Faulkner

Heinemann Library
Chicago, Illinois

Customer Service 888-454-2279
Visit our website at www.heinemannraintree.com

Produced for Heinemann Library by
White-Thomson Publishing Ltd

Consulting by David Judson
Designed by Tim Mayer
Artwork by William Donohoe
Printed in China by South China Printing Co. Ltd.

12 11 10 09 08
10 9 8 7 6 5 4 3 2 1

Library of Congress Cataloging-in-Publication Data
Faulkner, Rebecca.
  Beneath the surface / Rebecca Faulkner.
      p. cm. -- (Earth's final frontiers)
  Includes bibliographical references and index.
  ISBN 978-1-4329-0110-3 (lib. bdg.-hardcover) -- ISBN 978-1-4329-0116-5 (pbk.)
  1. Caves--Juvenile literature. 2. Speleology--Juvenile literature. I. Title.
  GB601.2.F38 2007
  551.44'7--dc22

      2007011229

Acknowledgments
The author and publisher would like to thank the
following for allowing their pictures to be reproduced in this publication: Alamy: **11** (Ricardo Siquera/Brazil Photos), **18** (Chris Howes/Wild Places Photography), **19** (Dyana), **34** (f1 online), **35** (Mark Boulton); Corbis: **6** (Arne Hodalic), **10** (Rainer Hackenberg/zefa), **13** (Theo Allofs/zefa), **14** (Vince Streano), **21** (Pierre Vauthey/ Sygma), **24** (Jonathan Blair), **25** (Tim Wright), **26** (Larry Lee Photography), **27** (Greg Smith), **28** (Liu Liqun), **33** (Aerie Nature Series, Inc), **36** (William A. Bake), **37** (Gerald Fauve), **39** (Michael St. Maur Sheil), **40–41** (Sergio Pitamitz); Digital Vision: **38, 41**; iStock: **8** (Daniel Hyams), **12** (Henry Lucentus), **15** (Vladimir Popovic), **16** (Rafa Irusta), **17** (Roger Asbury); NHPA: **30** (James Carmichael Jr.), **31** (Daniel Heuclin); Photolibrary: **9** (Pacific Stock), **22** (Photolibrary.com Australia), **23** (Index Stock Imagery); Science Photo Library: **29** (Brian Bell); Spellbound Tours, Waitomo Caves, NZ: **32**; Topfoto: **20** (Roger-Viollet).

Cover image (ice cave) courtesy of Hubert Stadler/Corbis.

CONTENTS

Words appearing in the text in bold, **like this**,
are explained in the glossary.

THE WORLD BELOW

▶ Earth's final frontiers are the most remote, inaccessible, and inhospitable regions on the planet. They are the areas that humans are still exploring and finding out about.

The world beneath Earth's surface is one of these final frontiers. Here, there are huge **caves** stretching for miles and containing amazing features and unusual life-forms. Here, there can also be found some of the most important **resources** that we rely on in our everyday lives. How to locate these resources and bring them to the surface is one of the greatest challenges we face today. All over the world, explorers and scientists are still discovering new things about the world beneath our feet.

This map shows the main areas where oil and **minerals** are mined in the world and some of the key cave locations.

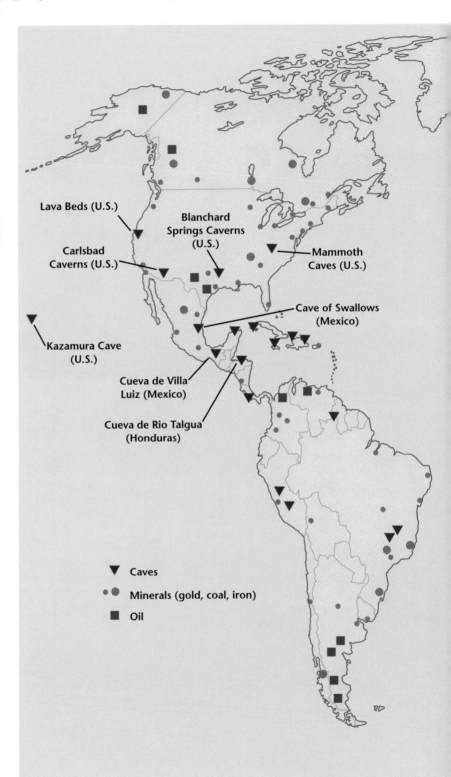

Lava Beds (U.S.)

Blanchard Springs Caverns (U.S.)

Carlsbad Caverns (U.S.)

Mammoth Caves (U.S.)

Cave of Swallows (Mexico)

Kazamura Cave (U.S.)

Cueva de Villa Luiz (Mexico)

Cueva de Rio Talgua (Honduras)

▼ Caves

● Minerals (gold, coal, iron)

■ Oil

Fingal's Cave
(Scotland)

Wookey Hole
(England)

Eisriesenwelt
Cave (Austria)

Blue Grotto (Italy)

Voronya Cave
(Georgia)

Lascaux Cave
(France)

Causse de
Gramat (France)

Sarawak Chamber
(Malaysia)

Easter Cave
(Australia)

Waitomo Caves
(New Zealand)

WHAT LIES BENEATH

What do you imagine you would find if you could travel deep underground beneath the surface of Earth? You would find a dark, mysterious world of soil and rocks. Many of these rocks would contain minerals, and some would be acting as natural storage containers for oil. Hollowed out into some of the underground rocks you would find **caves**.

UNDERGROUND PASSAGEWAYS

What do you think of when you imagine a cave? You may think of it as being a pitch-black, eerie place that is damp, dirty, and dangerous. You may think of it as a source of adventure and excitement, with dark passages leading to the unknown.

▼ *Caves are some of Earth's final frontiers because they are so inaccessible. Many of them can only be explored using special equipment.*

A cave is a place where rock has been worn away to leave a hollow cavity underground. Some are near the surface of Earth, while others are deep underground. Some are just big enough to crawl in, while others are made up of long, narrow tunnels.

Inside some caves, water carves out strange and amazing underground landscapes. It often creates spectacular underground waterfalls and lakes and produces beautiful rock formations. Strange creatures live in the depths of the darkness, and some caves contain the remains of ancient animals and even humans that lived thousands of years ago.

DEEP RESOURCES

Every day, whether you are at home, at school, or at work, you use Earth's resources. These are natural resources and are found beneath the surface on land and in the oceans. They include minerals, such as the salt you add to your food and the graphite in your pencil, as well as the important energy resources used for heating and lighting homes. These are coal, oil, and natural gas.

A FINAL FRONTIER

Humans have always loved to explore. Most of the world has already been discovered and mapped by the great explorers of the past, so it may seem that there is not much left to find. But people who are in search of adventure today can still find it. They just have to look a little deeper—beneath the surface of our planet.

A frontier is an area about which relatively little is known due to a combination of factors. These include its remoteness, inaccessibility, danger, and inhospitability. What lies beneath the surface is one of Earth's last unexplored realms . . . one of its final frontiers.

INSIDE EARTH

The inside of Earth is made up of different layers, like an onion. The **crust** forms the surface layer, and this is where you will find minerals, oil, and caves. This layer is very thin compared to what lies beneath, and it ranges in thickness from 6–44 miles (10–70 kilometers [km]). Below the crust is a thick layer called the **mantle**. This extends 1,800 miles (2,900 km) into Earth and contains extremely hot, molten rocks, up to 5,430°F (3,000°C). At the very center of Earth is the **core**, an even hotter liquid/gas furnace.

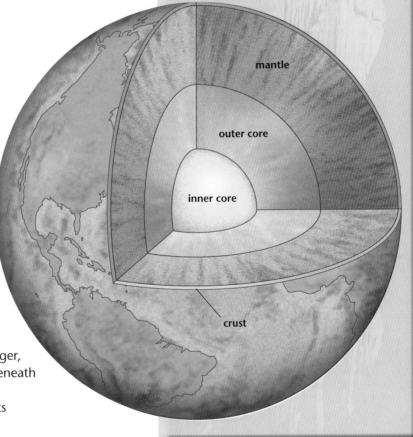

mantle

outer core

inner core

crust

THE WONDERFUL WORLD OF CAVES

Caves are found all over the world, but mostly in areas where there is **limestone** rock. They are continuously being formed and shaped, although it is a very slow process. Also, there are special types of caves formed in coastal areas by sea **erosion**, in **volcanic** regions through **lava** flows, and in cold lands.

SOLUTION CAVES

The caves that form underground in limestone rock are called solution caves. These are the most common type, forming about 98 percent of the known caves throughout the world. Although limestone is a hard rock, this does not prevent rainwater from dissolving it as it seeps into cracks in the rock. Over thousands of years, the underground rock is eaten away to form holes, passages, and eventually caves. This is called **corrosion**. The largest limestone area in the world is a huge region covering southwest China, north Vietnam, Cambodia, and Laos. There is probably more cave-forming limestone here than in all of the rest of the world put together.

SEA CAVES

In addition to rainwater, sea water can also erode the landscape. On the coast the waves constantly crash against the rocks. Over thousands of years, these rocks are eroded to form holes and cracks in the cliffs. These cracks are further eroded as the waves continue to batter the rocks. As more and more rock is worn away, the cracks grow into caves. A good example of a coastal cave is Smoo Cave, near Durness in the northwest corner of Scotland, on the Atlantic Ocean.

NATURAL REFRIGERATORS

How did people keep food cool before refrigerators were invented? In the past, ice caves were used as natural refrigerators. People who lived high in the Alps in Europe stored their food in them to keep it cool.

▼ *Sometimes a crack may form in the roof of a sea cave, and sea water can occasionally spurt out. This is called a* **blow hole**.

LAVA CAVES

Lava caves are tube-like cavities that form in lava after it has erupted from volcanoes. The lava that flows out of a volcano is very hot—over 1,800°F (1,000°C). As it flows over the surrounding land, the outer surface of the lava cools quickly as it meets the cooler air, and it hardens into rock. Underneath this hard outer surface, though, the lava is still hot and runny, so it flows away like a river. This lava river leaves a hollow, smooth-sided passage or tube underground. This is the lava cave.

Lava Beds National Park in California covers an area of 72 square miles (186 square km) and contains over 300 lava caves. These caves formed around 30,000 years ago when a volcano called Mammoth Crater erupted. The longest lava tube so far explored is Kazamura Cave, formed by Kilauea Volcano in Hawaii. It is 25 miles (41 km) long, 16 feet (ft.) (5 meters [m]) wide, and lies less than 66 ft. (20 m) below the surface.

ICE CAVES

An ice cave is a cave that has formed in rock, but is partly filled with ice. Many ice caves can be found in the Alps mountains of Europe and in cold areas of northern Canada and Russia, where the temperature drops below freezing in winter. The water inside the caves freezes, creating spectacular formations such as massive icicles and frozen waterfalls. Some caves are so cold that the ice does not thaw even in summer, so these are permanent features.

▲ *The Thurston lava tube forms part of the huge network of this type of cave in the Hawaii Volcano National Park.*

SMUGGLERS' CAVES

Caves and passages on the south coast of England used to be used by smugglers. Smugglers secretly brought goods illegally from mainland Europe to the United Kingdom. The smuggled goods included alcohol, tobacco, jewelry, and guns, and the smugglers hid them in caves. During World War II (1939–45), many of these caves were used as air-raid shelters during bombings.

THE ACTION OF WATER

Limestone is formed from the dead remains of tiny sea creatures that lived millions of years ago. When the sea creatures died, their bodies sank to the ocean floor. Over millions of years these tiny skeletons became crushed and hardened to form the limestone.

The process of forming caves in limestone is very slow. The reason that caves often form in limestone is because the rock can be dissolved by rainwater— it is a **soluble** rock. As rainwater travels through the atmosphere toward Earth's surface, it absorbs some of the carbon dioxide from the air. This turns the water into a weak acid called **carbonic acid**. This acid is very good at dissolving limestone.

Over thousands of years, the acidic rainwater eats away at cracks in the limestone, making them bigger and bigger. As the cracks become wider, more rainwater can get into the rocks below and continue the dissolving process underground. The cracks turn into holes and passageways. More and more water gets into the rock, so that underground rivers form, eroding the limestone as they gush through the passages. Eventually, after thousands of years, an underground network of caves will be created, linked by passageways.

▲ *On the island of Capri, off the coast of Italy, a beautiful limestone cave called the Blue Grotto is half underwater. Roman statues were found beneath the surface on the floor of the cave. These have been removed and taken to a museum.*

MAMMOTH CAVES

The longest cave system in the world is the Mammoth Cave system in Kentucky. The total mapped length of caves and passages is over 300 miles (500 km). The Echo River runs through the caves, about 330 ft. (100 m) below the ground. There are more than 200 caves in the cave system, with around 250 entrances to the caves. Cave explorers are still discovering new passages, and they often say that "there is no end in sight."

HOW DO CAVES GET SO DEEP?

A cave in Mexico called the Cave of Swallows is 1,300 ft. (400 m) deep. This is deep enough to cover the Empire State Building. But how do caves get so deep?

The depth of a cave is determined by the level of the **water table**. The water table is how deep beneath the surface the water flows into the rock. Below this level, the rocks are so full of water that no more can seep into them—they are **saturated**. The water therefore flows along the water table in an underground river, forming caves as it eats away at the limestone rocks.

▼ *Acidic rainwater erodes limestone rocks underground to form many cracks, passages, and caves.*

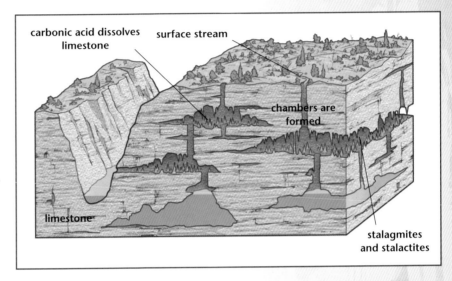

carbonic acid dissolves limestone

surface stream

chambers are formed

limestone

stalagmites and stalactites

The depth of the water table usually changes over time. When this happens, the river will carve out a new route. If there is a period of very little rainfall, called a **drought**, the water table will drop, the old caves will dry out, and new caves will be created by the water below. If the water table rises, due to heavy rain or a rise in sea level, the caves will become filled with water. The deepest cave in the world is the Voronya Cave, in Georgia, a country in southeast Europe. It is 7,120 ft. (2,170 m) deep.

▼ *The Gruta do Janelao ("Cave of Windows") in Brazil is one of the largest cave passages in the world. It is 200 ft. (60 m) high, and holes in the roof act like windows, letting light in. Explorers do not need a flashlight in this cave.*

CALCITE AND SPELEOTHEMS

As water trickles through limestone rocks, it dissolves a mineral called **calcite**. The flowing water can deposit this mineral to form many cave formations such as **stalactites** and **stalagmites**. Together, these formations are known as **speleothems**. Speleothems can form wherever mineral-rich water enters a cave. The rate at which speleothems form depends upon the amount and rate of water entering the cave, the amount of minerals in the water, and the temperature and **humidity** conditions in the cave.

▲ *All the different forms of speleothems can be seen in Carlsbad Caverns in New Mexico. Huge stalactites and stalagmites, like these, take thousands of years to form.*

STALACTITES AND STALAGMITES

As the mineral-rich water drips and dribbles from cave ceilings, tiny deposits of calcite are left behind. Over time these deposits gradually build up to form long, thin fingers of rock that hang down from cave ceilings like icicles. These are stalactites. The water that drips to the ground in caves may still contain some calcite. When this water **evaporates**, calcite deposits build upward from the cave floor to form pillars of rock called stalagmites.

Stalactites and stalagmites grow very slowly, at a rate of about 0.8 inch (in.) (2 centimeters [cm]) every 50 years, so you cannot watch them growing. They take thousands of years to form and can only grow when water drips through caves. Sometimes a stalactite and stalagmite may grow toward each other and eventually join up to form a solid column of rock.

WHO'S WHO

The Witch of Wookey Hole

Many caves containing spectacular speleothems are open to the public. Some of the formations are given names, such as the "Witch of Wookey Hole." This is a stalagmite in a cave called Wookey Hole in the United Kingdom that looks like a hunched, gnarled old witch. According to legend, a witch lived in the cave and cast evil spells on people. One day a brave monk decided to put a stop to this. He poured holy water over the witch and she turned to stone.

OTHER SPELEOTHEMS

Stalactites and stalagmites are not the only speleothems that can form in caves. Others include:

- Cave coral: A cave formation made of calcite that looks just like the coral you can find in tropical seas.
- Moonmilk: A white mineral deposit that looks like white cheese. It is a combination of calcite deposits and bacteria, and can be soft like plastic or dry and powdery.
- Straw stalactites: These form in the same way as stalactites and are long, hollow tubes that look like drinking straws. They are very thin, usually less than 0.2 in. (5 millimeters [mm]) across, which makes them very fragile. Waitomo Caves in New Zealand contain many clusters of straw stalactites, and in Easter Cave in Western Australia there is one that is over 20 ft. (6 m) long.
- Flowstone: This forms where calcite-rich water flows over cave ceilings, walls, and floors and leaves a deposit of calcite. These formations can be spectacular and often look like curtains or carpets. If there are **impurities** in the water, flowstone can look like bacon.
- Helicites: Delicate, curly calcite formations that can grow out in all directions from cave walls and ceilings. They can even grow on stalactites.

▼ *Speleothems can often be spectacular, like this formation, the Organ Pipes, found in Congo Caves, Western Cape Province, South Africa.*

RESOURCES FROM BENEATH THE SURFACE

Minerals are natural, solid materials that are formed deep in Earth's crust and mantle and combine together to form rocks. There are around 3,000 different minerals on Earth, including iron for steel making, salt for food, coal for fuel, and gold, silver, and diamonds for jewelry. Minerals from deep below the surface are very important for modern society. Most of the things we use every day at home, work, school, or play are made from minerals.

MINERAL MINING

Minerals are often buried beneath hundreds of feet of rock and have to be mined to **extract** them from Earth. There are two main methods of mining, depending on where and how a mineral deposit is found and how valuable it is.

Minerals that are found near Earth's surface can be extracted by blasting them out of the rocks in **open-cast mining**. Explosives are used to break up the rocks, and then machines strip away the soil and rock to reach the buried minerals below. Copper is often found close to Earth's surface, so is mined in this way.

▼ *Coal is usually buried in layers called seams. Near the surface, it can be mined by open-cast mining. Otherwise it needs to be extracted by deep mining.*

▲ *Diamonds are one of the rarest minerals extracted from deep underground. Because they are so rare, they are very precious and are often used in jewelry.*

Other minerals are found deep beneath the surface and have to be extracted by digging or blasting deep **shafts** and tunneling deep underground. Deep mining is more expensive than open-cast mining, so the minerals mined in this way must be valuable. Gold, silver, diamonds, and lead are mined like this.

REFINING

The minerals we want to extract are rarely found as pure, large lumps. They are usually mixed with other minerals that are of no use to us, so they need to be separated. This is called **refining**. Rocks that contain important or valuable metals are called **ores**. After the ore is mined, it is heated to a very high temperature or an electric current is passed through it. This separates the metal from the ore.

SMELTING

Heating the ore to very high temperatures to extract a mineral is called **smelting**. In this process rocks can be heated to more than 2,900°F (1,600°C). This method is used to separate iron from iron ore, for example. If an electric current is passed through an ore, this is called **electrolysis**. This method is used to separate aluminium from aluminium ore (bauxite).

DIAMONDS IN THE ROUGH

Diamonds are difficult to mine because they are usually found in very hard rocks. They are also very rare, so many tons of rock have to be mined to find only a few good-quality stones. Even in a diamond-rich mine in a country like South Africa, an average of 15.5 tons of rock must be removed to produce only 0.4 ounce (oz.)(1 gram [g]) of precious diamonds. This is why diamonds are so expensive.

GANGUE

Metal ores buried deep underground contain a lot of unwanted waste, as well as the minerals we want. This waste is called **gangue**. Some metals, such as gold and silver, are found uncombined in Earth's crust. This is very useful because it means they do not need to be separated from an ore.

FUELS FROM THE DEEP

Coal, oil, and natural gas are **nonrenewable fossil fuels** and are the most important energy resources on Earth today. They are found deep in Earth's crust and are formed over millions of years from the remains of dead plants and animals. When they are burned, energy is released as heat and light.

Because oil is a liquid, it does not remain where it formed. It seeps through cracks in the rocks until it reaches a layer of **impermeable** rock, through which it cannot pass. This is called an **oil trap**. The oil remains in this trap in a layer of **porous** rock, which holds the oil like a sponge holds water. Natural gas also collects in traps and is often found with oil.

HOW ARE OIL AND NATURAL GAS EXTRACTED?

In order to extract oil and natural gas, geologists need to find these oil traps. Engineers can then drill deep into Earth's crust, through thousands of feet of solid rock, to release the oil and gas so that it will rise up to the surface. If the oil trap is located under the ocean floor (**offshore**), an oil rig needs to be constructed in order to drill down into the ocean floor to extract the oil and natural gas.

An oil rig can be floating, or it can have very long legs that reach all the way to the ocean floor. From these offshore rigs, drills can reach oil and gas deposits up to 20,000 ft. (6,000 m) below the ocean floor. The drills used for extracting oil have teeth made of diamond. This is the hardest mineral we know of and can cut through the surrounding rock at a rate of 525 feet per hour (160 meters per hour).

A LIMITED RESOURCE

Fossil fuels are nonrenewable, which means they will eventually run out, because they are being extracted from Earth and used at a much faster rate than they are being replaced. It took nature one million years to create the amount of fossil fuels being burned on Earth today in just one year. We are now developing **renewable** energy resources such as **solar** power and wind power to help solve this problem.

▼ *Every time you travel by plane, you are using fuel made by plants and animals that lived millions of years ago.*

When oil comes out of the ground, it is thick and black and is called **crude oil**. It is transported to oil **refineries** by **pipelines** or huge oil tankers. Crude oil cannot be used, so in a refinery it is made into gasoline, diesel, kerosene, and other fuels that are used every day.

▲ *This pipeline in the cold frontiers of Alaska is used to transport oil to oil refineries.*

WHAT ARE FOSSIL FUELS USED FOR?

Wherever you are, at school or at home, on a plane or in a car, things made from fossil fuels are all around you. We use coal, oil, and natural gas to make the fuel needed to drive cars, buses, trains, and airplanes, as well as for cooking, lighting, and heating. Oil is also used to make many of the other things we need for modern life, such as plastics, fertilizers, paint, soap, shampoo, and make-up. Oil is even added to food as a preservative and coloring.

Fossil fuels supply around 90 percent of the energy we need to live our everyday lives. Oil is the most important fossil fuel, and it supplies 40 percent of the world's energy. It is sometimes given the name "black gold" because it is so valuable. Natural gas provides 20 percent of the world's energy. Taken together, oil and natural gas provide twice as much energy as coal.

EXPLORING THE DEPTHS

The world is full of unexplored caves. Some may contain untouched mineral formations that have been silently growing for thousands of years. New caves are being discovered and explored all the time.

CAVE EXPLORERS

The only way to find out about caves is to look inside them. The underground world of caves is very different from the world above ground. It is dark and strange, and full of excitement and danger. This is why it is such an attractive area to explore.

In their own words ..

"It's not an adrenaline game, it's something else—a full challenge to the human spirit." Cave explorer Bill Stone explains the thrill of investigating unexplored caves, *National Geographic*

▼ *Cave exploration requires special equipment and often involves getting cold and wet.*

Exploring caves can be dangerous. It is easy to lose your way in an unmapped maze of underground passages. The route back to the surface may become blocked by a sudden rockfall or flooding if there is heavy rain. Some passages can be very steep, or even vertical, while other passages might be filled with water. Explorers therefore need to be climbers and divers in order to overcome all these difficulties—and everything has to be done by flashlight. So, what makes people venture into this dangerous frontier? It is all for the excitement of finding an unknown world and the scientific discoveries that can be made.

▲ *Speleologists create maps of the underground world that can be used and added to when exploring caves and passageways.*

CAVE SCIENCE

Scientists who study caves are called **speleologists**, and the study of caves is called **speleology**. Caves are like natural museums. They contain evidence of past climates, **extinct** animals, and long-dead humans. These remains may lie untouched for thousands of years until they are discovered by explorers.

Speleologists enter the mysterious underground world to study how it has formed and how creatures can survive there. They make maps of caves, describing the rock types and formations found. They try to find new, undiscovered caves by studying geological maps for clues as to what lies below. These clues can include streams that suddenly disappear or reappear, or hollows that should contain lakes but do not. These all suggest that the water must be going underground and possibly forming caves.

Speleology is an exciting science because there is still much to be learned. New cave discoveries are being made all the time, due to new methods of exploration and better maps. For example, cave diving has greatly expanded the number and types of cave that can be studied. This means that caves filled with water can now be explored, providing a wealth of new information.

▲ *In 1939 this early French cave explorer, Norbert Casteret, followed an underground river in Labouiche cave in France in an inflatable life raft.*

EARLY CAVE DISCOVERIES

Caves have been found on every continent, even in Antarctica. Exploring the polar regions is exceptionally difficult, though—they are another one of Earth's final frontiers because of the extremely harsh weather conditions. A number of early explorers managed to overcome all the difficulties that caves can present to make some amazing discoveries.

The French lawyer Edouard Alfred Martel is known as "the father of speleology" because he was one of the most daring cave explorers of his time. Between 1888 and 1914 he explored beneath the surface of parts of Europe, descending into shafts up to 525 ft. (160 m) deep, a record for the time. In 1889 Martel descended the 330-ft. (100-m) deep Padirac shaft in the Causse de Gramat in France and discovered an underground stream. Together with his cousin, he followed the stream in an inflatable life raft for about 1.2 miles (2 km).

NATIVE AMERICAN DISCOVERIES

The huge system of interconnected caves that make up Mammoth Caves in Kentucky was first discovered more than 200 years ago by Native Americans searching for a white mineral called gypsum to use as medicine. We know this because fossil humans have been discovered in the caves, including one man who was found beneath a 6-ton boulder. Even these early humans discovered that exploring caves can be dangerous.

EARLY ART

Lascaux Cave in France is famous for the prehistoric paintings it contains. These are thought to have been painted around 15,000 years ago. Four boys discovered the Lascaux Cave in 1940 by accident when their dog fell in it. The cave walls display more than 600 paintings, including 50 paintings of bulls, as well as other animals such as deer, bears, rhinos, and an animal that looks like a unicorn. These early artists used charcoal, plant juices, and animal blood to paint pictures of animals on the walls of caves. The paintings tell us that these prehistoric humans spent most of their time hunting for food in order to stay alive.

Exploring caves can tell us a lot about our history. Thousands of years ago, caves were important for shelter. Native Americans used Blanchard Springs Caverns in Arkansas as shelters, and in Australia many **aboriginal** people lived in caves. We know that early humans lived in caves because explorers have discovered stone and bone tools, paintings, and even human skeletons in them.

CLUES TO THE PAST

Fossils are found in rocks and are the remains of ancient plants and animals that died millions of years ago. They provide clues to life in the past because they tell us about the animals that used to inhabit caves. Many of these plants and animals may now be extinct, so if there were no fossils we would not even know that they had existed.

▼ *Because the original paintings in Lascaux Cave in France were being destroyed by tourists, an exact replica of the cave has been built nearby. Tourists can now only visit this replica cave.*

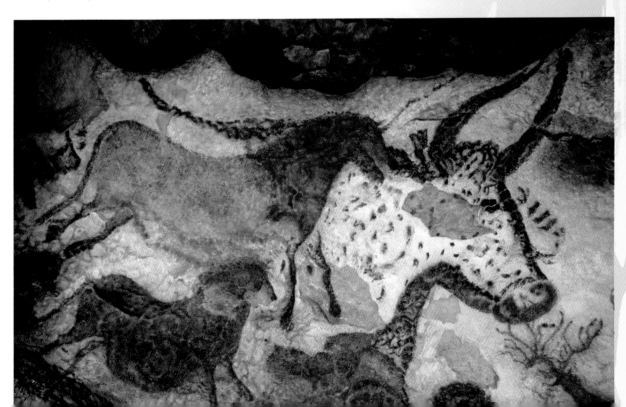

RECENT CAVE DISCOVERIES

Speleologists and explorers are still discovering new caves. One of the most famous recent cave discoveries was made in 1981, beneath previously unexplored thick mountainous rainforest in Sarawak on the island of Borneo in Malaysia. British cavers were following an underground river called the Clearwater River through a dark, winding passage, when suddenly it opened out into a huge underground chamber. The cave was so enormous they could not see the walls when they shone their flashlights into it. It took them 12 hours to explore and survey it completely.

This is the largest single cavern ever found. It is called the Sarawak Chamber and has been hollowed out by the Clearwater River eroding sideways across the limestone. It is 2,300 ft. (700 m) long, up to 1,300 ft. (400 m) wide, and about 230 ft. (70 m) high. This cave is so big that it could contain more than 20 football fields. The area is still being explored today, in the hope that an even larger cavern will be found.

DIVING DANGERS

Cave diving is a challenging and potentially dangerous activity. Divers have to navigate through narrow passages, strong currents, and of course the constant darkness. Two divers died when they were trapped in an underwater cave after part of the roof collapsed, blocking their only exit route.

▼ *Until 1981 Sarawak Cavern remained hidden beneath thick tropical rainforest. The huts in this picture give an idea of how huge the cavern is. There may be more undiscovered caves in this area.*

AN UNDERGROUND WONDERLAND

A cave called Lechuguilla Cave, in Carlsbad Caverns National Park in New Mexico, was first explored in 1986. The strange, beautiful formations found there are so delicate that this cave is not open to the public, and only speleologists can enter it. It contains enormous stalagmites, up to 20 ft. (6 m) long, growing up from the cave floor, and huge numbers of fragile straw stalactites hanging down from the ceiling like curtains made of icicles. The two types of speleothems often meet and form spectacular columns of rock. Smooth flowstone covers the cave walls and makes them look like they have been coated in marble. Delicate, needle-like helicites grow in all directions, creating a beautiful underground wonderland.

AN ANCIENT CEMETERY

In 1994 in Honduras, in Central America, cavers discovered the Cueva de Rio Talgua (Cave of the Talgua River) near the edge of the rainforest. They found it by accident when they slipped through a crack in the limestone rocks above it. To their amazement, the cave contained hundreds of human bones, the skulls of which sparkled in their flashlights. The skulls sparkled because, over thousands of years, calcite-rich water dripping from the cave roof had covered them in tiny calcite crystals. This inspired the cave's nickname, "Cave of the Glowing Skulls."

FUTURE CAVE EXPLORATION

Deep underground are countless unexplored caves, just waiting to be discovered. The future is bright for cave exploration because caves are continuously being formed. New passages are being eroded out of the rocks and new formations are being deposited, drop by drop, on cave walls, floors, and ceilings. The sounds of dripping water are everywhere. Cavers are constantly searching for new caves. New techniques and new technology mean that they can search for more remote caves, deeper caves, and even caves that are now underwater through cave diving.

▲ *Carlsbad Caverns in New Mexico contain the deepest cave in the United States. The Lechuguilla Cave is 1,600 ft. (490 m) deep. It is famous for the rare and amazing speleothems it contains— in perfect condition.*

MINERAL EXPLORATION

Minerals are found all over the world, but only in certain areas are they found in sufficient quantities for economic extraction. Most minerals form deep inside Earth as hot liquid material that then cools and hardens to form rock. Because different minerals are found in different rocks, geologists study the rocks of an area to figure out if important minerals are likely to be found there.

Minerals such as copper and lead can sometimes be found as **mineral veins**. These are like sheets of minerals that are found in cracks in rocks. They form when hot, mineral-rich water rises up through Earth's crust and enters a crack in the rocks.

EARLY MINERAL EXPLORATION

In the past, mineral exploration was called **prospecting**. Prospectors traveled around **panning** for gold and other minerals in rivers. In 1848 a large amount of gold was discovered in California. This led to the "gold rush," in which around 300,000 people traveled to the area to find their fortune. Gold worth billions of dollars was recovered, leading to great wealth for some; others, however, returned home with little more than they started with.

▼ *An explosion blasts the soil and rocks away to help create a new mine shaft for coal mining in Secunda, South Africa.*

EXPLORATION TODAY

Today, geologists use **satellite images** to look at the geology of an area in order to determine if minerals can be found there. A satellite image is a photograph taken from space that covers a huge area. If the geologist had to study the same area by walking around on the ground, it would take months and involve walking for hundreds of miles!

From a satellite image, geologists will figure out where minerals are likely to be found. They will then use **geophysical** techniques to try to find out if the minerals are actually there. Some of these techniques allow geologists to detect minerals buried deep underground, since they can "see through" the overlying rocks.

One of these techniques is used to find a mineral called magnetite, which is an ore of iron. Magnetite is naturally magnetic, and geologists can find it using a technique called **magnetic surveying**. An airplane carrying special equipment will fly over the area, and the magnetic survey equipment can pinpoint where any magnetic rocks are hidden underground. These rocks are likely to contain iron.

Despite the use of modern technology, mineral exploration is still very difficult, and it is likely that many mineral deposits lie unexploited, hidden deep beneath the surface, just waiting for us to find them.

▲ *Aircraft like this are used in mineral surveying. The wires measure changes in the magnetic field as the plane flies over the land and indicate where valuable minerals might be found.*

SALT OF THE EARTH

A huge salt mine, which lies 1,200 ft. (366 m) beneath the city of Detroit, Michigan, operated until 1983. The mine, formerly owned by the International Salt Mine Company, spreads out over more than 1,400 acres (565 hectares) and had 50 miles (80 km) of roads. Today, the mines are open for public tours.

OIL AND GAS EXPLORATION

Oil and gas are found in more than half the countries of the world, but most stores, called **reserves**, are very small. The largest gas reserves in the world are found in Russia, and the largest oil reserves are found in Saudi Arabia in the Middle East. Although much of the land surface of Saudi Arabia may look barren and lifeless, lying deep beneath this desert surface lies one-quarter of all Earth's oil reserves.

Oil and gas are usually buried deep in Earth's crust, underneath layers of solid rock. Geologists therefore have to work hard to find them. The rewards of finding oil and gas are huge, and countries that have a lot of reserves can become very rich. Because oil is so valuable, very few regions of Earth remain truly unexplored. Oil has been found on every continent except Antarctica. This is because at the moment Antarctica is protected from oil exploration by the Antarctic Treaty. Even this final frontier may soon be breached, as it comes under increasing pressure to explore and exploit it.

▲ *A huge oil drill is mounted on a platform and used to drill deep down through thousands of feet of solid rock in an attempt to find oil.*

Oil exploration began over 100 years ago in the United States. Early drilling was carried out in places where oil seeped up to Earth's surface and on the basis of guesswork. These early attempts to find oil were often unsuccessful. The United States is often regarded as the birthplace of the modern oil industry. The first successful attempt to drill for oil was made by Edwin Drake in Pennsylvania in 1859. He drilled to a depth of 69 ft. (21 m) and collected the oil in a bathtub. His efforts led to the growth of the oil industry, but did not make him rich.

EXPLORATION TODAY

Today, oil is big business. Companies drill for oil and gas from the hot deserts of the Middle East to the frozen deserts of Siberia. Modern technology means we can even pump oil and gas from thousands of feet below the ocean floor. New reserves are still being found. China, Egypt, and Thailand have all recently become oil-producing countries.

Finding oil is a mixture of science and guesswork. Geologists use the latest modern techniques, such as satellite images and **seismic surveys**. They study satellite images to look at the geology of an area to decide if oil and gas are likely to be found below the surface. Seismic surveying is a technique that can "see through" the surface rocks to show the rock layers beneath. A small explosion is made just below ground, and **shock waves** from this explosion travel through the underground rocks. Geologists use special instruments to measure these shock waves, and can use this information to figure out where oil traps are likely to be found.

▼ *The results from a seismic survey are used to create a seismic chart like this one. This shows the different rock layers deep beneath the surface and helps geologists locate oil and gas.*

FUTURE RESOURCE EXPLORATION

Despite modern technology, the search for oil is full of uncertainties, and finding oil is still very difficult and expensive. The only way to be sure that oil is below the surface is to drill. If all the clues point to oil and gas below, small rigs will be built and test drilling will take place to see if there is actually anything there.

Developments in technology mean that the mining industry today employs specially equipped planes, helicopters, and satellites to find potential mining sites. Scientists have discovered potato-sized lumps called **nodules** buried in the sediment on the floor of the Pacific Ocean, which contain important minerals such as manganese, cobalt, and nickel. In the future it may be possible for remote-controlled machines to collect these nodules and bring them to the surface.

▼ *As the need for more oil increases, more and more rigs are being set up all over the world. These oil rigs are in the Shaanxi Province of China.*

▲ *This engine is the very latest in mining technology and is used to drive the huge mining machinery.*

Like fossil fuels, minerals are nonrenewable resources, and so if we use too much of them they will eventually run out. Because we are using up a lot of Earth's minerals, mining companies spend more than $1 billion a year on exploration, research, and development trying to find new sources. In the future we will need to seek out minerals from greater depths underground, from the ocean floor, and even from beyond Earth, such as mining on the moon, asteroids, or other planets.

OIL AND GAS

Because we are using up oil and gas faster than they can be replaced, more reserves need to be found. The search for oil has extended into more remote parts of the world, both onshore and, increasingly, offshore. In particular there is also the possibility of drilling for oil and gas deeper on the ocean floor, using remote-controlled oil rigs.

Oil has recently been discovered in porous rocks called **oil shales** and **tar sands**. These have soaked up oil like a sponge, and new technology means that the oil contained within them can be piped up to the surface. This technique is very expensive at the moment, but in the future we may need to extract more of this type of oil as other reserves run out.

LIFE IN THE UNDERGROUND WORLD

You may think that nothing could possibly live in the cold, dark, underground world, or you may think that nothing would want to live there. But animals can make their homes in the most unlikely places. Camels can survive in hot, dry deserts, and penguins can cope with Antarctic ice. So why shouldn't life be found deep in the darkest cave?

LIFE IN THE DEPTHS OF DARKNESS

The animals found deep inside caves are called **troglodytes**. These creatures spend their whole lives in caves, on the damp, rocky walls and floors. They have to cope with life in the cold darkness. They never see daylight and never set foot on the surface of Earth. Troglodytes include poisonous scorpions, Huntsman spiders, giant beetles, eyeless millipedes, and blind white fish.

SNOT AND SALIVA

Some amazing creatures have been discovered that live in caves, including white snakes that hang from cave walls and attack bats as they fly past. In a cave called Cueva de Villa Luiz ("Cave of the Lighted House") in Mexico, strange slimy, white bacteria known as "snot-tites" hang from the walls and ceilings. They look like stalactites, but have the consistency of "snot," or mucus. Cave swiftlets are birds that live on cave walls in southern Asia and build their nests out of saliva. The saliva is thick, white, and sticky, and it hardens when it dries.

These creatures have adapted to life in this dark world. They are often blind, or almost blind—such as blind daddy longlegs and blind beetles. Instead of sight, troglodytes develop their sense of touch to help them find their way around and search for food.

Troglodytes also tend to be colorless, white or **translucent** (almost see-through)—such as the translucent cave cricket or translucent cave crab. This is because body color does not help cave creatures hide or recognize each other, when they cannot see each other anyway.

SEE-THROUGH SWIMMERS

In the dark, cool waters of underground rivers, there are blind, translucent cave fish. These fish do not grow eyes, but they manage to dart around at high speed through the pitch-black water of the rivers without bumping into each other. They have nerve endings all over their bodies that sense movement in the water. This means they can feel their way around and follow movements to obtain their next meal of insects.

▲ *The blind cave fish has a pinkish tinge to it because its skin is translucent, meaning you can see the blood inside it.*

WHO'S WHO

Other cave creatures
Caves are alive with creepers and crawlers, swimmers and fliers. There are over 100 species (types) of animals lurking in the cracks and crevices of caves. Other than troglodytes, cave creatures include:

● **Trogloxenes**: Creatures that spend part of their life in caves, such as bats.

● **Troglophiles**: Animals that primarily live in caves and will rarely venture above ground, such as cave crickets.

GLOWING INSECTS

Glow worms are beautiful and unusual animals that live in the darkness of caves, lighting up the walls and ceilings with tiny specks of light. Glow worms are not actually worms. They are the **larvae** of tiny flies called fungus gnats.

The rear end of the glow worm produces the glow, due to a chemical reaction inside its body. This glowing rear end will attract insects, which will then become food for the glow worm. When an insect flies toward the glowing light, it will become tangled in long, sticky threads dangling from the glow worm like fishing lines, and the hungry glow worm will eat it for its next meal.

▲ *Waitomo Caves in New Zealand are famous for their glow worms. The ceilings of the caves often shimmer and glisten with the blue-green light made by thousands of glow worms.*

FLYING MAMMALS

The smallest bats weigh about as much as a pencil and are the same size as your hand. There are around 950 different types of bats, but most cave bats are small and look like mice with wings. They live in groups called colonies, and they do not live permanently in caves because they are trogloxenes. They sleep in caves during the day, hanging from the roof, and then go out in search of insects for food at night.

Carlsbad Caverns in New Mexico contain over half a million bats. When it gets dark, around 5,000 bats a minute zoom out of the caves. They are expert fliers, twisting and turning through the air as they chase insects through the darkness. Bats are mammals, not birds, so their wings are made of thin, tough skin, rather than feathers. They wrap their wings around their body to keep warm when sleeping in damp caves.

Bat droppings are called guano, and they pile up to form a thick carpet on cave floors. Other cave dwellers cannot afford to be fussy eaters, and the guano provides food for millions of dung-eating cave insects.

WHO'S WHO

Small and ferocious

- Vampire bats can be found in caves in South America. They get their name because they bite animals and lick their blood. They do not kill the animal with their bite, but they can pass on a disease called rabies.

- The world's smallest bat is the bumblebee bat of Thailand. It is the smallest mammal in the world and weighs less than a penny.

ECHOLOCATION

You may have heard the saying "as blind as a bat." Bats have eyes and are not completely blind, but just like us, they cannot see in the darkness of a cave. How then, do they fly through the maze of passageways without bumping into things? The answer is they "see" in the dark through hearing—a process called **echolocation**. Bats make continuous high-pitched sounds, called **ultrasounds**, that are too high for human ears to hear. The echoes from these sounds bounce off obstacles in the bat's path, such as cave walls, trees, buildings, or even people. These echoes tell the bat where any obstacles or insects are and enable the bat to fly around them or catch them for food.

▼ *Mexican free-tailed bats live in caves in the southern United States and Mexico. The largest colony is at Bracken Cave, near San Antonio, Texas.*

CONSERVING THE FRONTIER

Caves are popular tourist attractions in many countries. When visiting caves, it is important not to touch or tread on any cave deposits or disturb them in any other way, because once they are destroyed, formations that may have taken thousands of years to form are lost forever.

CAVING

Many people like to explore caves for the excitement and danger or the challenge of getting from one end to another. The sport of caving is a popular activity, but it can be dangerous. It may involve descending many hundreds of feet into a cave down a rope or ladder, wiggling and squeezing through narrow gaps in the rocks, crawling along low passageways, wading through water, or simply experiencing the total darkness and silence of the cave.

All cavers need to be familiar with cave-rescue techniques in case of an accident or emergency situation. This could include an injury caused by a slip or a rockfall, a person getting stuck in a narrow passage, or a sudden flood cutting off the way back to the surface.

Many caves and cave creatures are in danger of being destroyed by disturbance from thousands of tourists, pollution from garbage, poisonous chemicals from parking lots, and waste from cities.

▼ *In tourist caves such as these in Spain, walkways lead visitors through silent chambers filled with strange and beautiful calcite formations that are lit up using artificial lighting. It is important that tourists do not touch any of these delicate formations.*

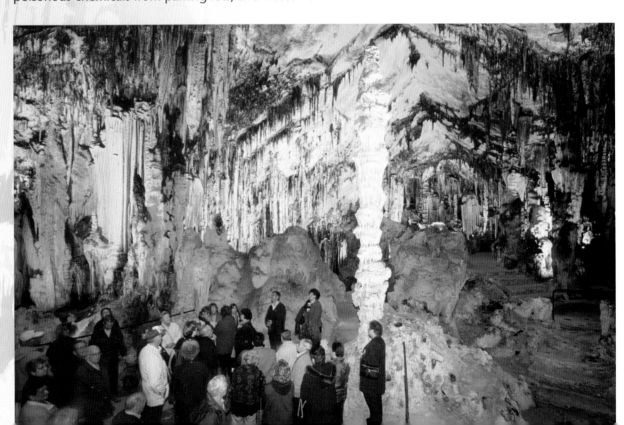

A FRAGILE ENVIRONMENT

The environment within a cave deep underground is very finely balanced. Humans can easily destroy this natural balance in many ways, often without realizing it:

- A clumsy tourist may tread on delicate cave formations that have taken millions of years to form, thus destroying them forever.

- A speleologist may damage a speleothem when attempting to find out how old it is.

- A careless caver may grab a stalactite to pull himself onto a ledge and either break it off completely or cause it to turn black due to the natural oil on human hands.

- Creating walkways and lighting up areas for tourists may disturb the natural habitat of cave animals.

- Even minor disturbances, such as a noisy group of schoolchildren, can affect cave animals with a low **resilience** to change, forcing them to search for a home elsewhere.

▲ *Even getting into a cave can be difficult and dangerous. Cavers have to be very careful about their own safety and about the environment they are exploring.*

In their own words ...

"Leave nothing but footprints, take nothing but pictures, kill nothing but time."
Caving Association motto

Anyone entering a cave must be careful not to affect the fragile environment within. Throwing trash on the cave floor can kill cave wildlife, and a broken stalagmite cannot be put back together. Future visitors will want to see unspoiled caves as much as you do.

◄ *In Blanchard Springs Caverns in Arkansas, cave walkways and lighting have been carefully designed to have minimum impact on the cave environment.*

CAVE CONSERVATION

Some damage done to a cave may heal in time, but it will happen very slowly, over thousands of years. Some damage will be permanent; a delicate speleothem may be lost forever, and unique, cave-adapted animals can be unintentionally wiped out by a single caver. For these reasons, caves and the unique biological and geological resources they contain need to be protected.

In the United States today, many caves have been awarded National Park status. This means they are protected. Carlsbad Caverns, Mammoth Caves, and Lava Beds have all been made into National Parks. In Blanchard Springs Caverns in Arkansas, the natural air inside the caves is near 100 percent humidity, so special doors have been fitted to all cave entrances to prevent dry air from outside the cave from getting in and altering the **microclimate** of the cave. The size of tour groups is also limited. In the United Kingdom, some caves and cave areas have been given SSSI (Site of Special Scientific Importance) status, which gives them legal protection.

Vandalism of cave formations was so bad in Carlsbad Caverns that alarm systems have been installed. The alarm is controlled by an infrared system, and if anyone touches any of the formations, the alarm will sound. In order to protect the delicate formations in particularly fragile caves, some cave systems have now been closed to all visitors except speleologists carrying out research. This is the case with Lechuguilla Cave in New Mexico.

RULES FOR RESPONSIBLE CAVING

- Cave with care.

- Stay on marked routes.

- Avoid touching or damaging formations.

- Do not disturb cave wildlife.

- Do not pollute the cave; leave nothing behind.

- Take nothing but photographs.

▼ Speleologists carry out research in a cave in Iceland. There are many caves here formed by volcanic eruptions, but in order to protect the creatures and formations in the caves, many are only accessible to scientists.

Caves are a unique and very special part of our natural environment. Because of their slow and gradual formation over thousands of years, amazing calcite formations can be created and intriguing creatures can find a home. We need to ensure this final frontier is carefully preserved for the benefit of future cavers, scientific research, and the general public.

MINING AND THE ENVIRONMENT

In order to extract minerals from the ground, it is inevitable that an area of the land surface will be disturbed. Soil has to be removed to open up a mine, thus destroying plants and disturbing animals. Sometimes whole communities of people may need to be moved to make way for a new mine. Open-cast mining in particular is very destructive to the natural landscape. Deep mining may have a less unsightly effect on the landscape, but since tunnels are blasted out underground, this can lead to **subsidence** of the land above.

While a mine is operating, waste rock and dust can pollute the land around the mine. If the chemicals used in the mining operations or the waste rock get into rivers, they can pollute water supplies in the region. If water is contaminated, people cannot use it for drinking, cooking, or washing. When a mine closes, ugly waste piles and dangerous mine shafts are left behind.

In the past, little attention was given to the protection of the environment, and there were certainly no environmental regulations in place. Miners led dangerous lives working long hours underground. They did not worry about destroying the natural landscape or contaminating water supplies with waste products.

▼ *Once production at this mine comes to an end, the site will be turned into farmland once more, so you would never know a mine had existed here.*

SYNTHETIC MINERALS

Scientists have learned how to make some minerals artificially for use in industry. The minerals are grown in a laboratory and are called **synthetic minerals**. Synthetic silicon is used for making computer chips and synthetic emeralds are made for use in jewelry.

CLEANING UP

Today, environmental protection is a key issue. It is important to find a balance between the need for mineral extraction and the need to protect the environment. Scientists and miners need to find and extract mineral resources with the least possible disruption to our environment.

▲ Waste water from a coal mine in China enters the Jiu River without any form of filtration or attempt to remove contaminants.

The mining industry is developing cleaner technologies and new processes to ensure that mining activities are conducted in an environmentally responsible way. During mining operations, soil embankments are built to reduce the visible effects of the mine, and waste is treated to reduce pollution.

There are strict laws that mean land disturbed by mining must be returned to its natural state or turned into parkland. Once mining is finished, mining companies must return the soil to the site, landscape the area, and plant it. Open-cast mine pits can also be filled with water to create artificial lakes.

As we use more and more minerals, they are becoming harder to find. We need to conserve our dwindling supply of minerals by using less of them, by recycling them, or by developing new technology to create substitutes.

POISON RIVER

In 1995, 106 million cubic feet (3 million cubic meters) of poisonous cyanide waste from a gold mine in central Guyana, in South America, spilled into the large Essequibo River for five days. All the fish in the river died, and many people developed skin rashes and respiratory problems. Despite the pollution, the mining company was not punished because Guyana has no environmental protection law.

HARMFUL GASES

When fossil fuels are removed from the ground and burned, they release harmful gases called sulfur dioxide and nitrogen dioxide into the air. When it rains, some of the rainwater absorbs these gases to produce **acid rain**. This can damage buildings, kill trees, and harm fish in rivers and lakes.

Burning fossil fuels also releases a gas called carbon dioxide into the air. This is a **greenhouse gas**, which means it traps heat, just like a greenhouse in a garden. As the population of the world has increased, more and more people need fuel, and so more and more fossil fuels are burned. This means that the amount of carbon dioxide in the air has increased. More carbon dioxide traps more heat, and so Earth has become warmer. This is known as **global warming**, and most scientists confirm that this will lead to ice melting at the North and South Poles, causing flooding in some countries. It may also result in an increase in extreme weather events such as storms and change where plants can grow.

OIL SPILLS AND BLOW OUTS

Oil and gas are often found in remote places, so they need to be transported to refineries where they can be converted into forms we can use. On the way to refineries, oil can sometimes spill from a pipeline or oil tanker. This causes water or land pollution. If a tanker spills oil into the ocean, the oil floats on the surface as a thick, black **oil slick**, killing fish and seabirds and polluting the water.

OIL SLICKS

In 1999 an oil tanker called *Erika* spilled about 2.6 million gallons (10 million liters) of oil into the ocean off the coast of France. The oil slick killed over 100,000 seabirds. In an even bigger disaster, in 1989 an oil tanker called *Exxon Valdez* spilled 13 million gallons (49 million liters) of oil into the ocean off the coast of Alaska.

▼ *Could this melting iceberg be a result of using too much fossil fuel?*

FACTS AND STATISTICS

RECORD-BREAKING CAVES

Record	Cave	Location	Vital statistics
Deepest cave	Voronya Cave	Georgia (in Europe)	7,120 ft. (2,170 m) deep
Longest cave	Mammoth Caves	Kentucky, U.S.	Over 300 miles (500 km) long
Largest cave	Sarawak Chamber	Borneo, Malaysia	2,300 ft. (700 m) long, 1,310 ft. (400 m) wide, 230 ft (70 m) high

AMAZING CAVES

Cave	Cave type	Location	Distinguishing features
Blue Grotto	Limestone	Capri, Italy	Half underwater
Carlsbad Caverns	Limestone	New Mexico, U.S.	Stalactites and stalagmites
Waitomo Caves	Limestone	New Zealand	Straw stalactites and glow worms
Easter Cave	Limestone	Western Australia	Straw stalactite over 20 ft. (6 m) long
Wookey Hole	Limestone	United Kingdom	Stalactites and stalagmites
Lascaux Cave	Limestone	France	Prehistoric paintings
Cueva de Rio Talgua	Limestone	Honduras	Hundreds of human bones
Cueva de Villa Luiz	Limestone	Mexico	Unique, slimy cave creatures
Lava Beds	Lava cave	California, U.S.	300 lava tubes
Kazamura Cave	Lava cave	Hawaii, U.S.	25-mile (41-km) long tube
Eisriesenwelt Cave	Ice cave	Austria	1,000-ft. (300-m) high ice wall

Sometimes, when oil trapped underground is released by drilling, it explodes out of the ground in what is called a **blow out**. Not only does this waste precious oil, it also pollutes the surroundings. In 1992 in Uzbekistan, in Central Asia, engineers drilled into oil under so much pressure that it exploded hundreds of feet into the air and continued to gush out for 62 days.

WHAT ARE THE ALTERNATIVES?

Because of all the pollution caused by fossil fuels, we need to limit their use and use other forms of energy. You can help to conserve fossil fuels by switching off electrical items such as lights, computers, and air-conditioning systems when they are not in use. You can also reuse or recycle many of the things you would normally throw away, such as glass bottles and newspapers. Reusing plastic bags saves fossil fuel because less is needed to make more products. Glass made from recycled glass uses one-third less fuel than glass made from raw materials.

▲ *Oil slicks kill over half a million seabirds each year.*

FOSSIL FUELS

We are using fossil fuels much faster than they are being replaced, so sooner or later we will run out. Scientists think that Earth's reserves of oil will last for around 35 years, natural gas will last for 50 years, and coal will last for around 240 years.

2040: Oil will run out.

2060: Natural gas will run out.

2250: Coal will run out.

Scientists have discovered ways of using other natural resources, such as the sun and the wind, to make electricity. These exist in unlimited quantities and will never run out, so they are called renewable resources. Solar panels are used to capture the sun's energy, and the wind turns wind turbines to generate electricity. These renewable resources provide us with energy that we can continue to use forever, and they do not pollute the environment like fossil fuels.

GLOSSARY

aboriginal people who have lived in a country or region since ancient times; often used to specifically refer to the native people of Australia

acid rain rainwater that has been polluted; it kills plants and wears away buildings

blow hole crack in the roof of a coastal cave through which sea water sometimes spurts

blow out oil exploding out of the ground

calcite mineral found in limestone that is dissolved by water and deposited elsewhere to form speleothems

carbonic acid weak acid created when water and carbon dioxide mix; this acid can dissolve limestone

cave place where rock has been worn away to leave a hollow cavity underground

cavern large chamber within a cave

core central layer of Earth

corrosion when rock is worn away by the action of water

crude oil unrefined oil from the ground, before it is made into a usable form

crust thin surface layer of Earth

drought period when there is very little rainfall

echolocation process by which bats "see" in the dark through hearing echoes

electrolysis passing an electric current through an ore to separate the metal from it

erosion when wind or water wears away rocks

evaporate change from a liquid state to a vapor

extinct when an animal or plant has been hunted or used to the point that it no longer exists

extract take something from the ground, such as minerals

fossil fuel naturally occurring fuel, such as coal, oil, or natural gas, formed by the fossilized remains of plants and animals

gangue unwanted part of an ore

geophysical physics relating to Earth and its environment

global warming effect of increased carbon dioxide trapping heat and warming Earth

greenhouse gas gas such as carbon dioxide that traps some of Earth's outgoing heat

humidity amount of moisture in the air

impermeable rock that does not have spaces to allow oil or natural gas to pass through

impurity something in a substance that does not occur there naturally

larva young stage of an insect's life cycle

lava molten rock erupted from a volcano

limestone rock formed from the remains of tiny sea creatures that lived millions of years ago

magnetic surveying searching for magnetic minerals using aircraft with special equipment

mantle hot layer of Earth beneath the crust

microclimate climate of a small space or area that differs from that of the surrounding area. Most caves have a microclimate.

mineral substance found in Earth that can be mined—for example, gold and iron

mineral vein layer rich in minerals found in cracks cutting through rocks

nodule lump found within sedimentary rocks that can contain useful minerals

nonrenewable resources that will eventually run out, such as coal and oil

offshore not on land; in or under the ocean

oil shale porous rock that has soaked up oil like a sponge; the oil can be extracted from the shale

oil slick area of oil floating on the surface of the ocean after a spill

oil trap layer of rock that oil and natural gas cannot pass through

open-cast mining method of shallow mining in which rocks are blasted and machines strip away the soil and rock to reach the buried minerals below

ore mineral that contains an important metal

panning process of sifting through small rocks to find gold

pipeline large pipe built to carry oil from a drilling site to a refinery

porous full of holes; able to soak up liquids

prospecting old-fashioned term meaning to search for minerals

refinery place where coal, oil, or natural gas is changed into forms that can be used

refining process of separating useful minerals from those that are of no advantage to humans

renewable resources that will always be available and are constantly replenished, such as the sun and wind

reserve amount of something, such as oil or natural gas, in a certain place, which can be extracted

resilience ability to recover quickly from damage or disturbance

resource anything that can be used to human advantage. Natural resources include oil and minerals.

satellite image photograph taken from a satellite in space

saturated so full of water that no more can be absorbed

seismic survey technique that can "see through" the surface rocks to show the rock layers beneath

shaft vertical passageway to a mine or cave

shock wave movement of Earth generated by an explosion

smelting process of heating an ore to very high temperatures to extract a metal or mineral

solar relating to the sun

soluble something that will dissolve in water, such as limestone rock

speleologist scientist who studies caves

speleology study of caves

speleothem calcite deposits in caves; stalactites and stalagmites are types of speleothem

stalactite thin, icicle-shaped finger of rock that grows as water drips from cave ceilings

stalagmite pillar of rock that builds upward when water drips onto a cave floor and evaporates

subsidence sinkage or collapse of the ground